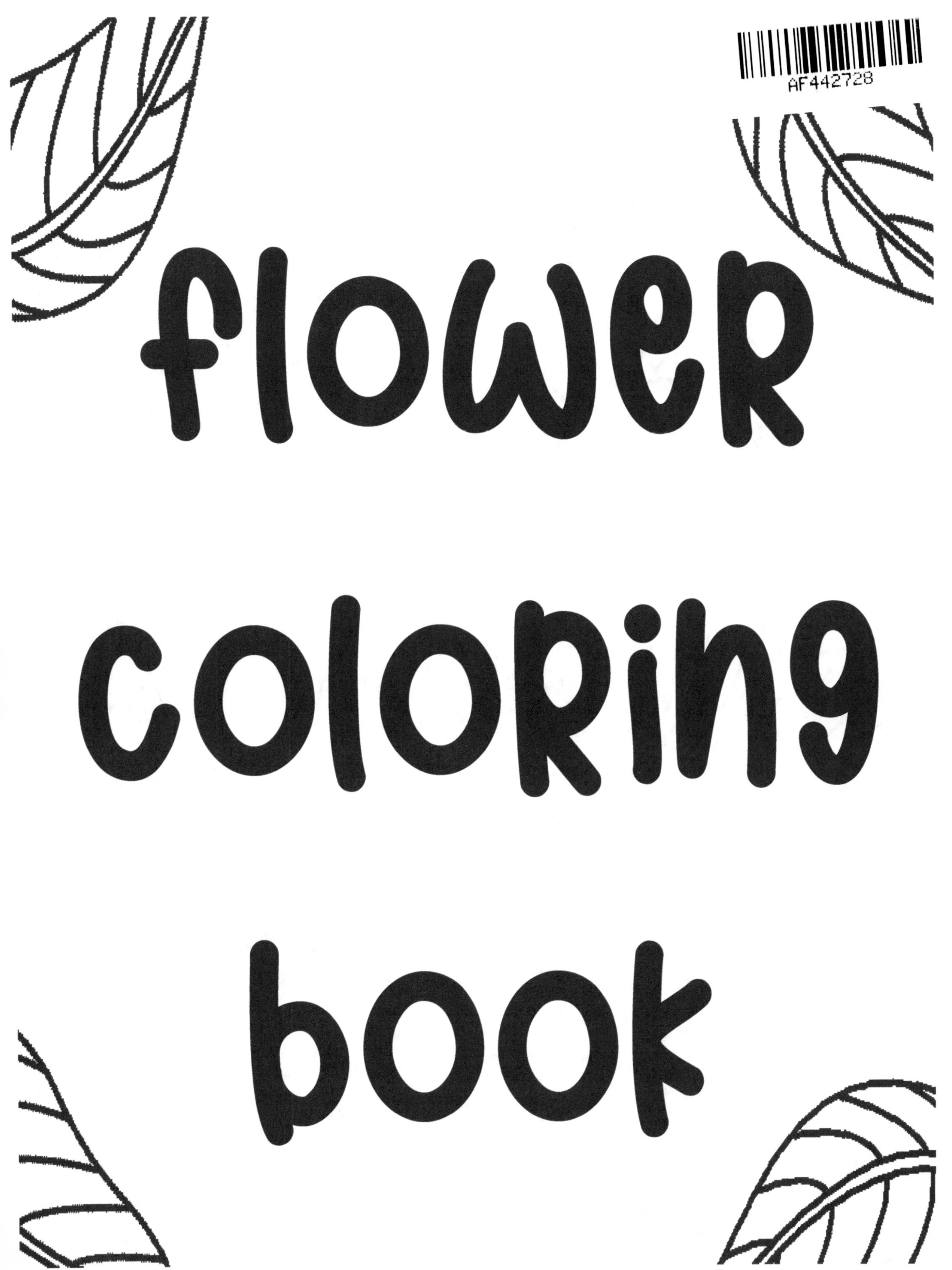

flower coloring book

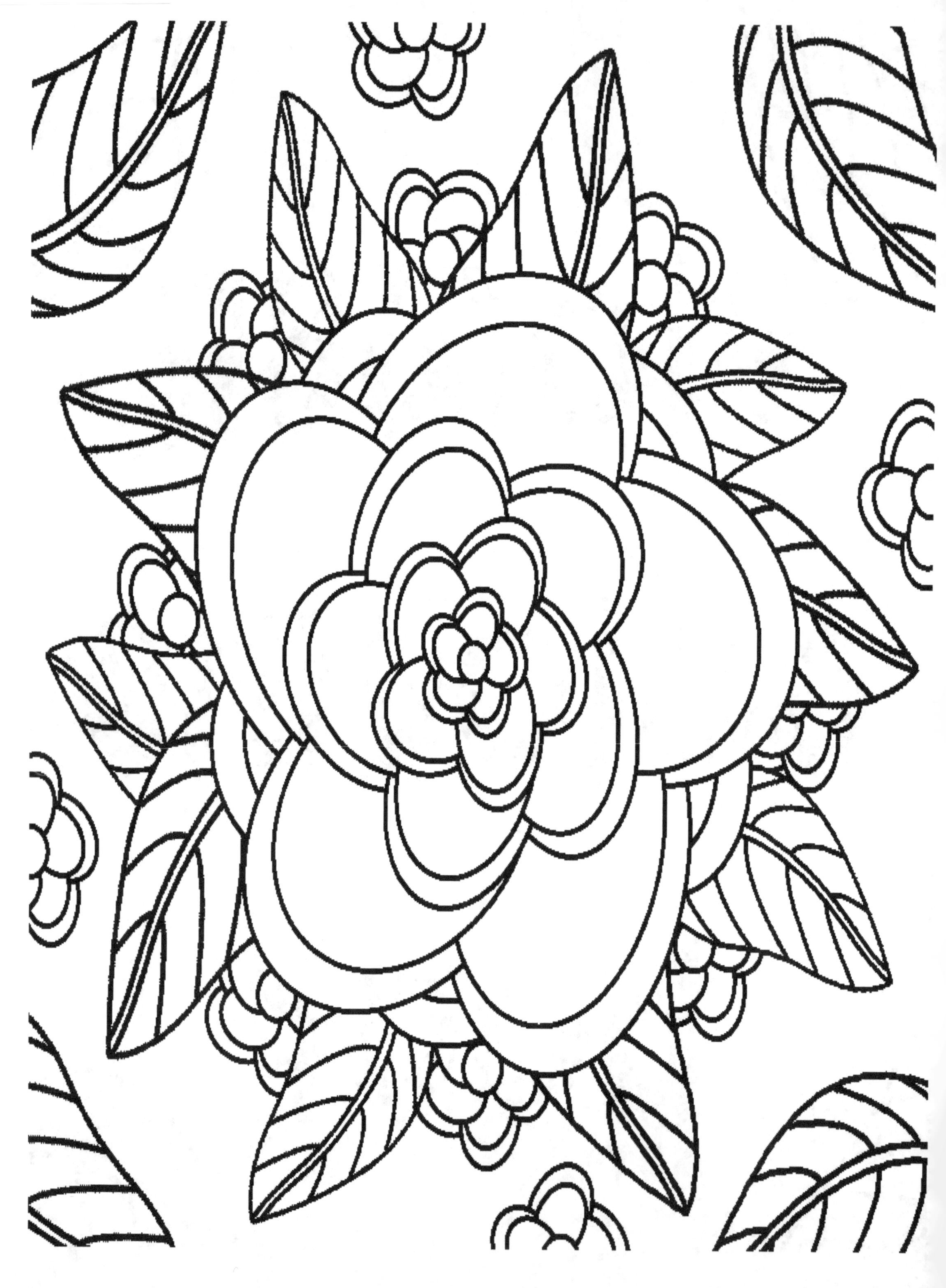

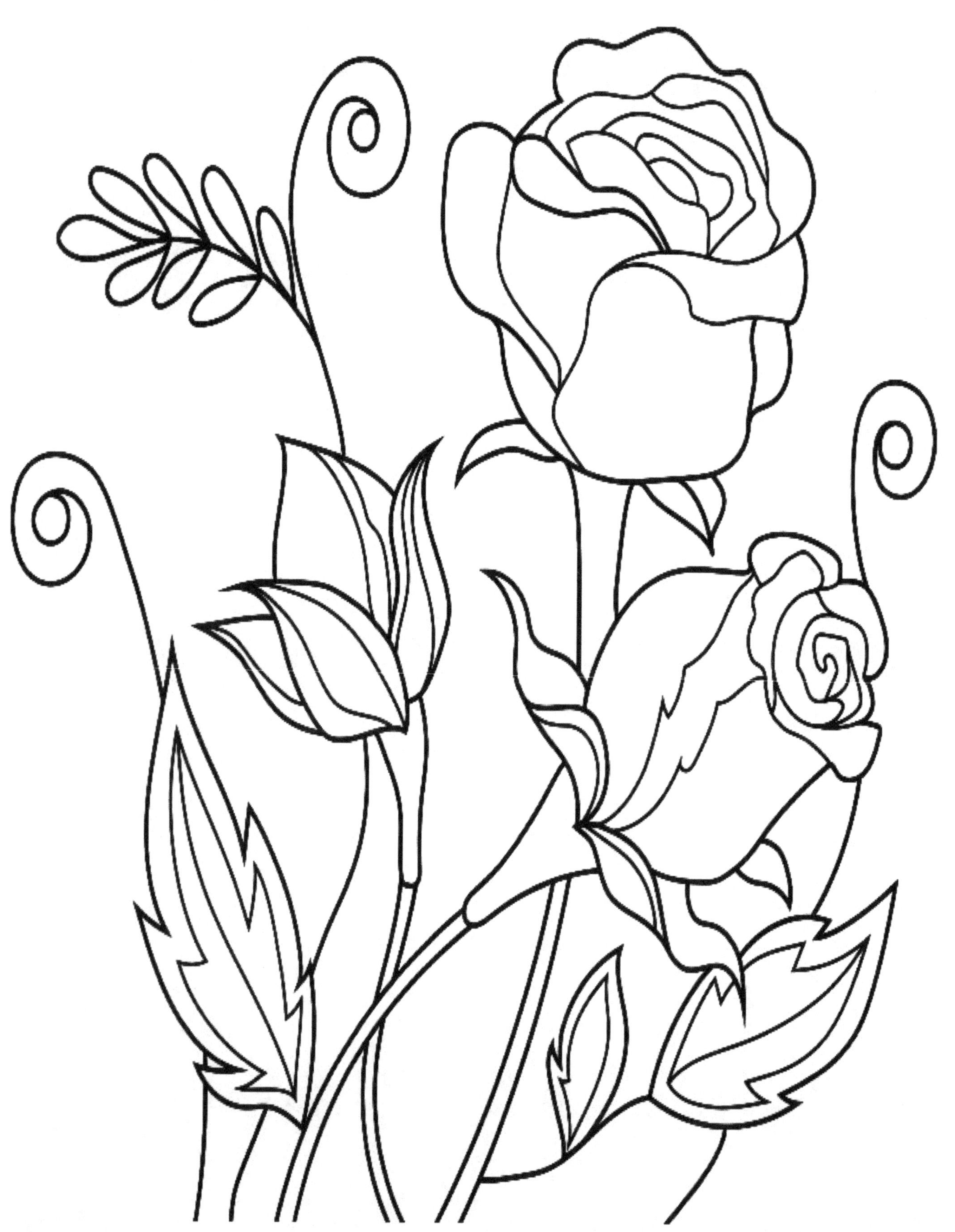

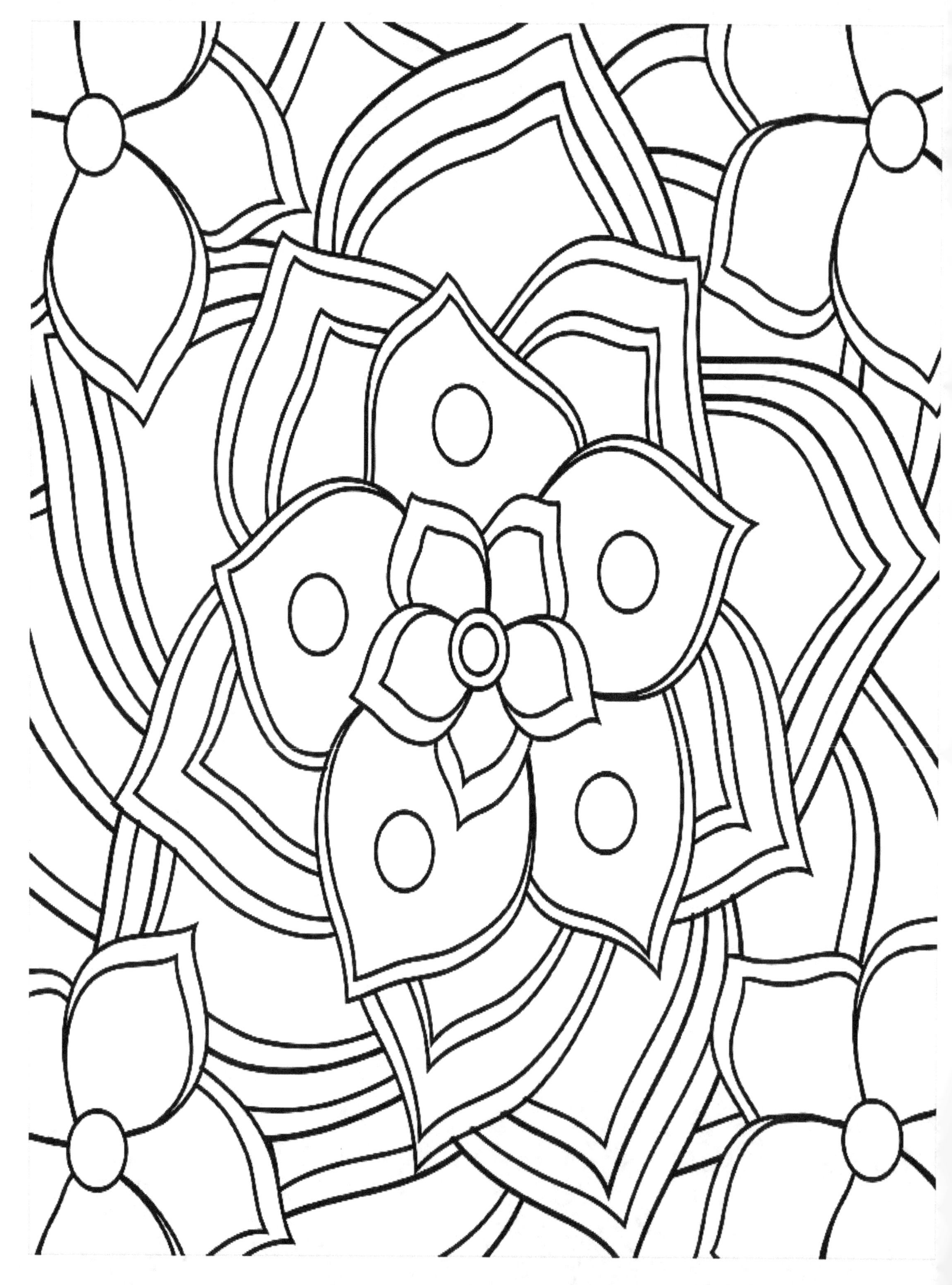

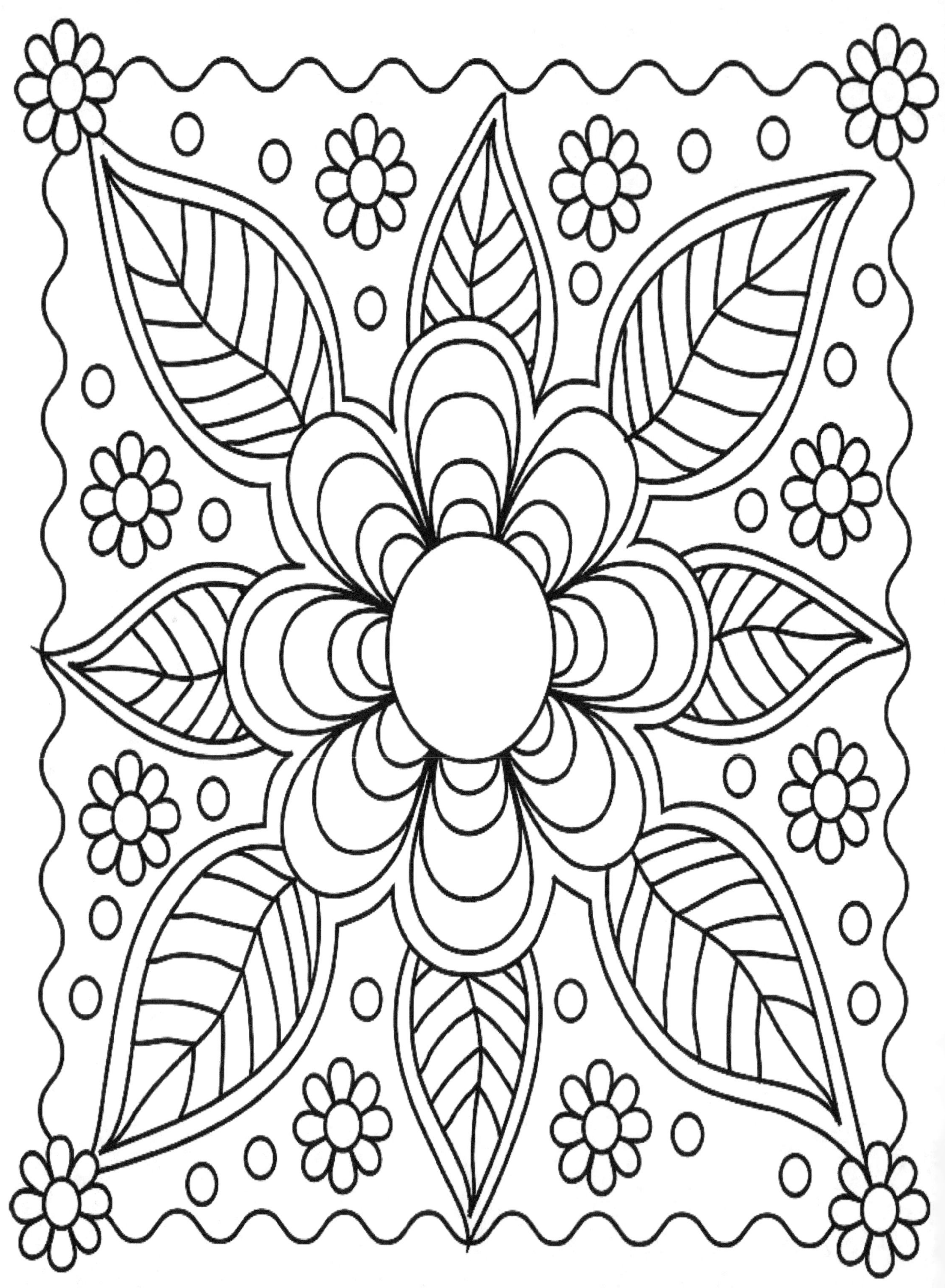

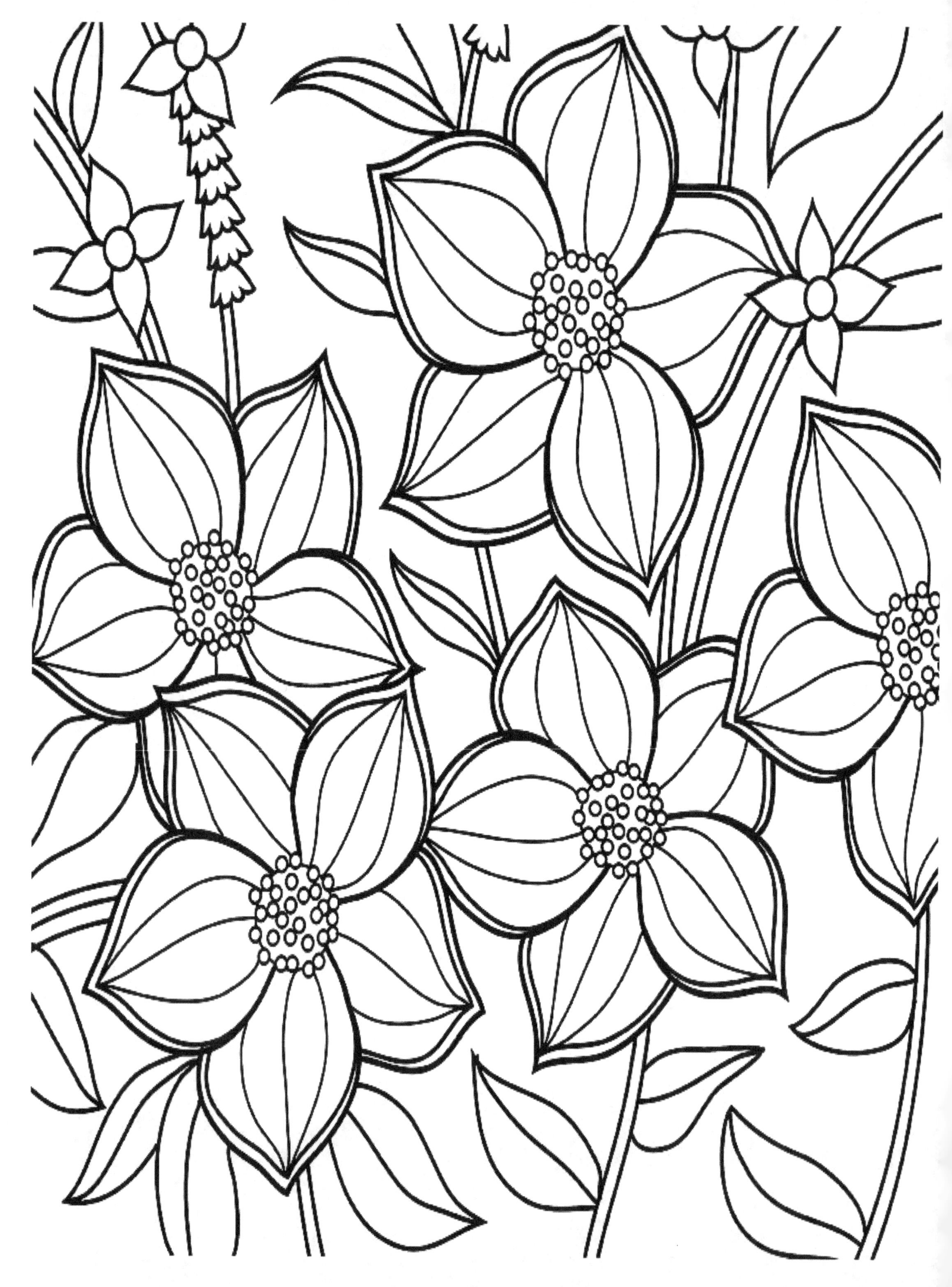

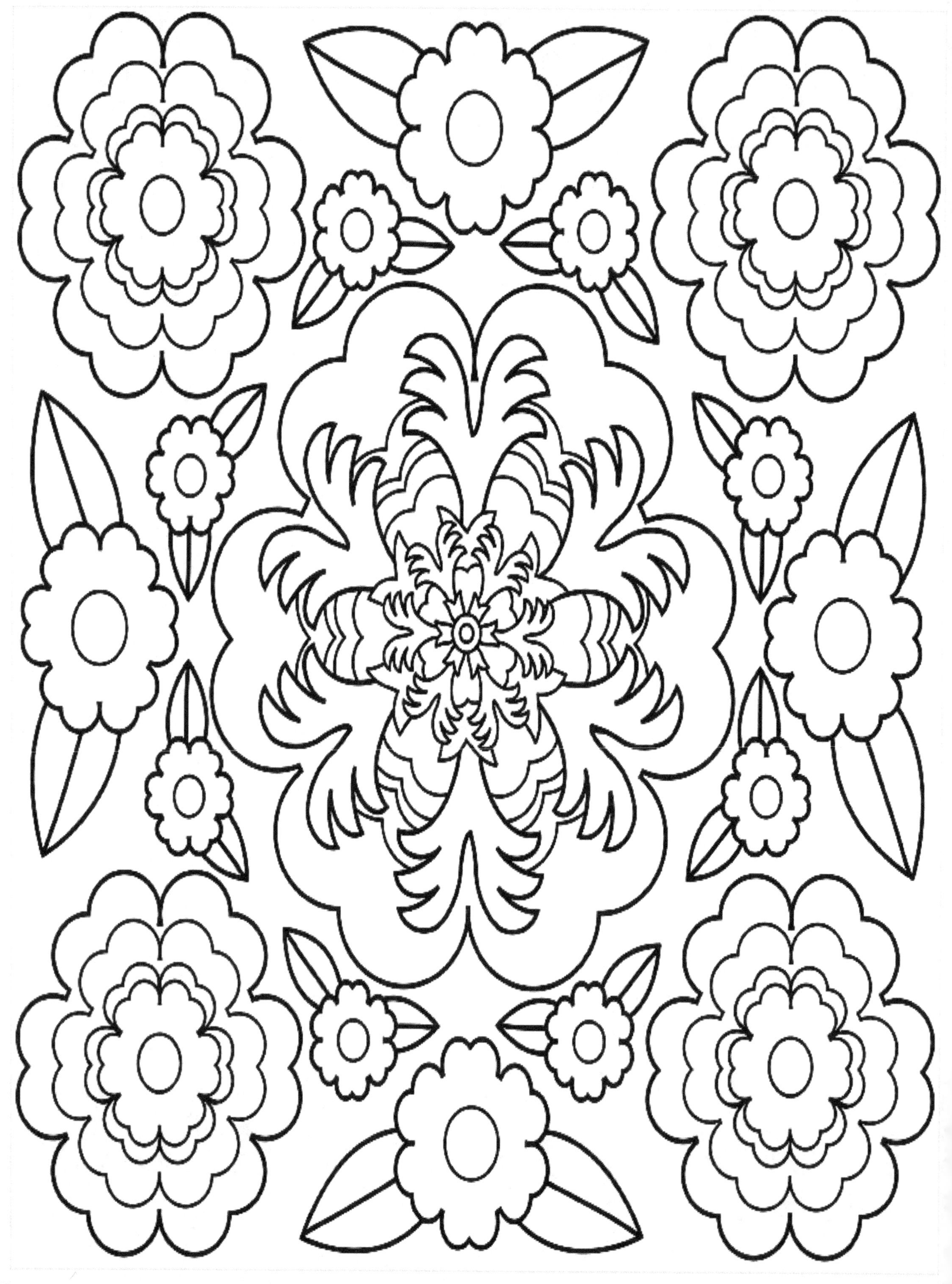

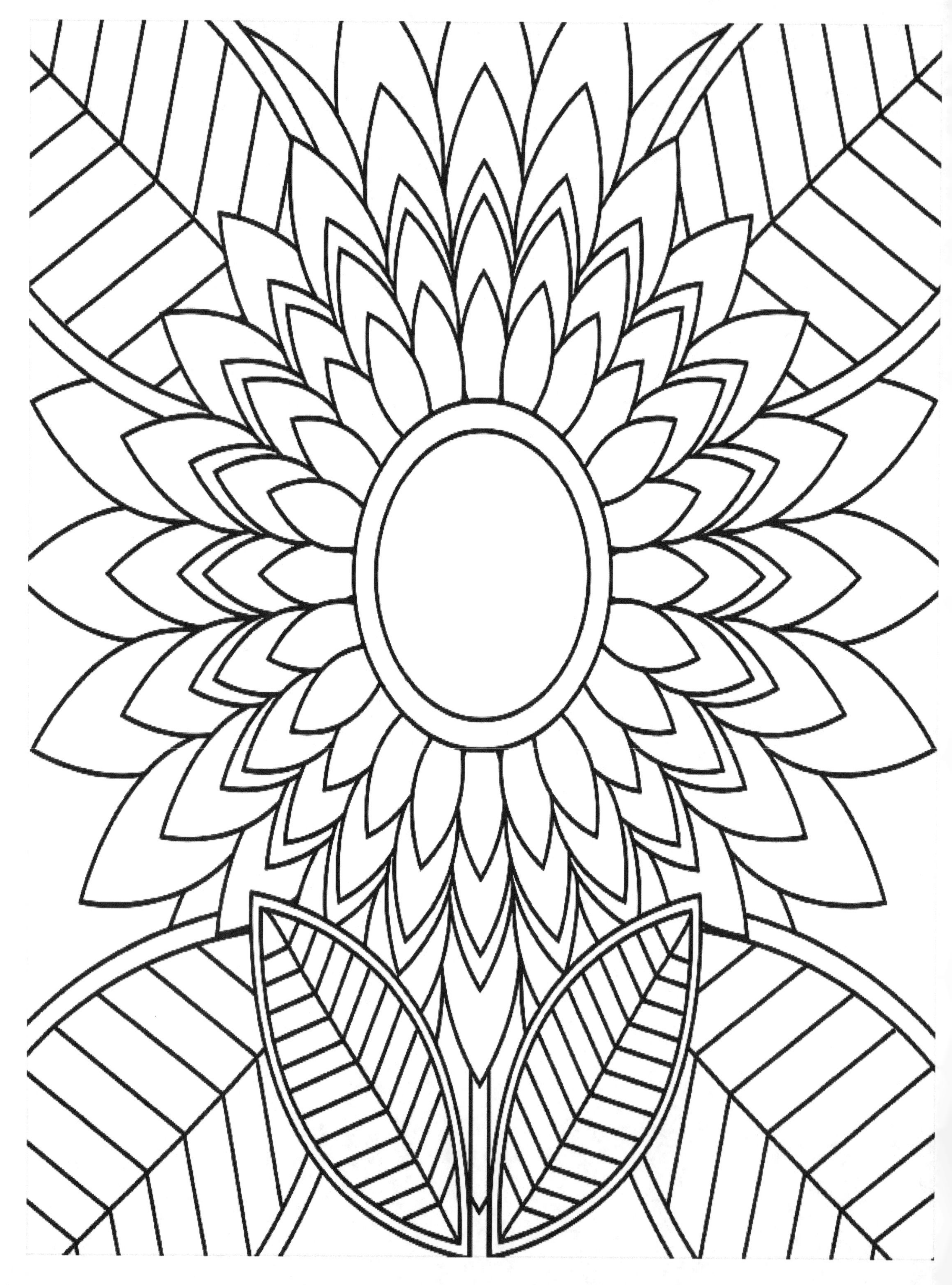

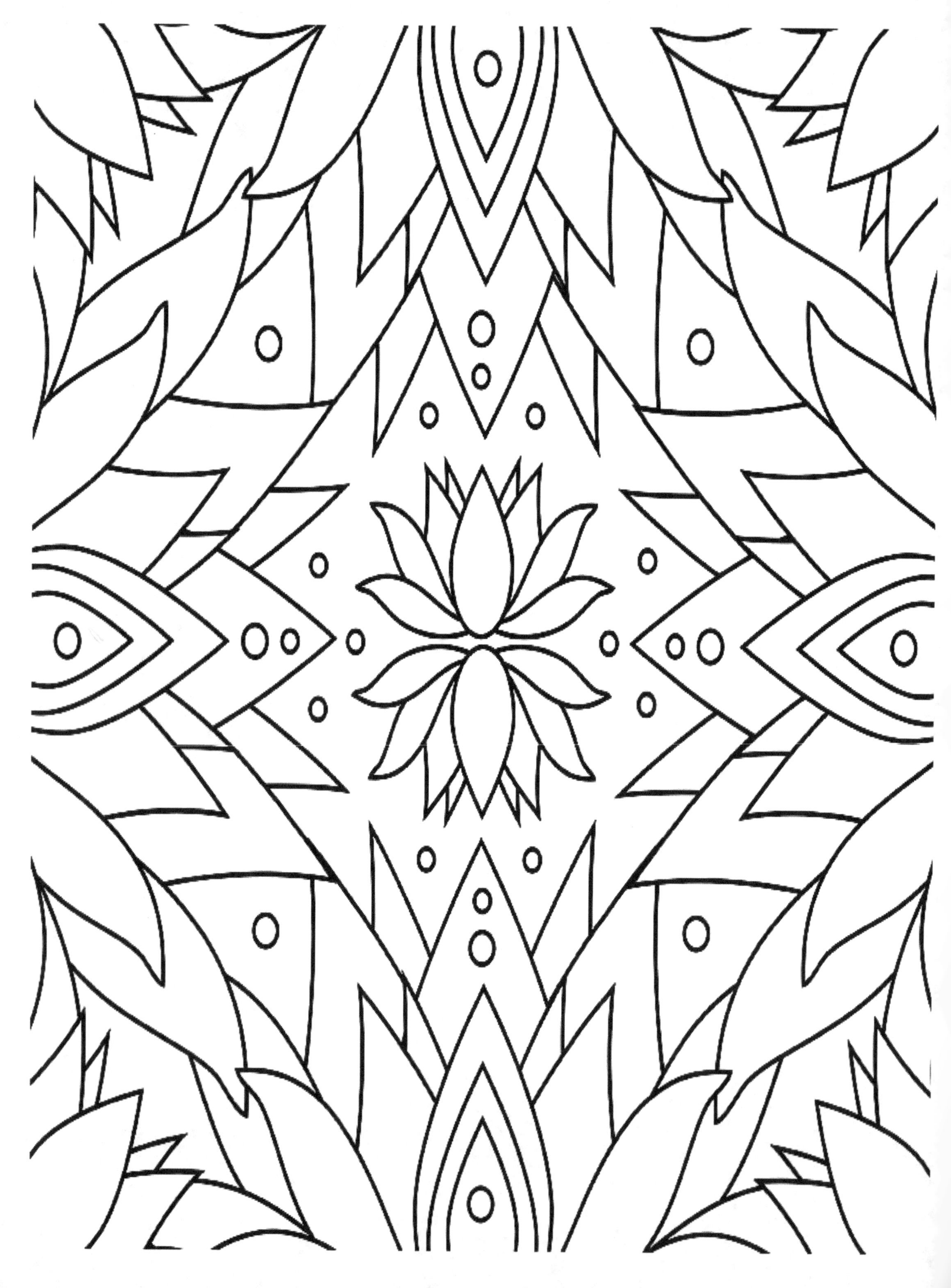

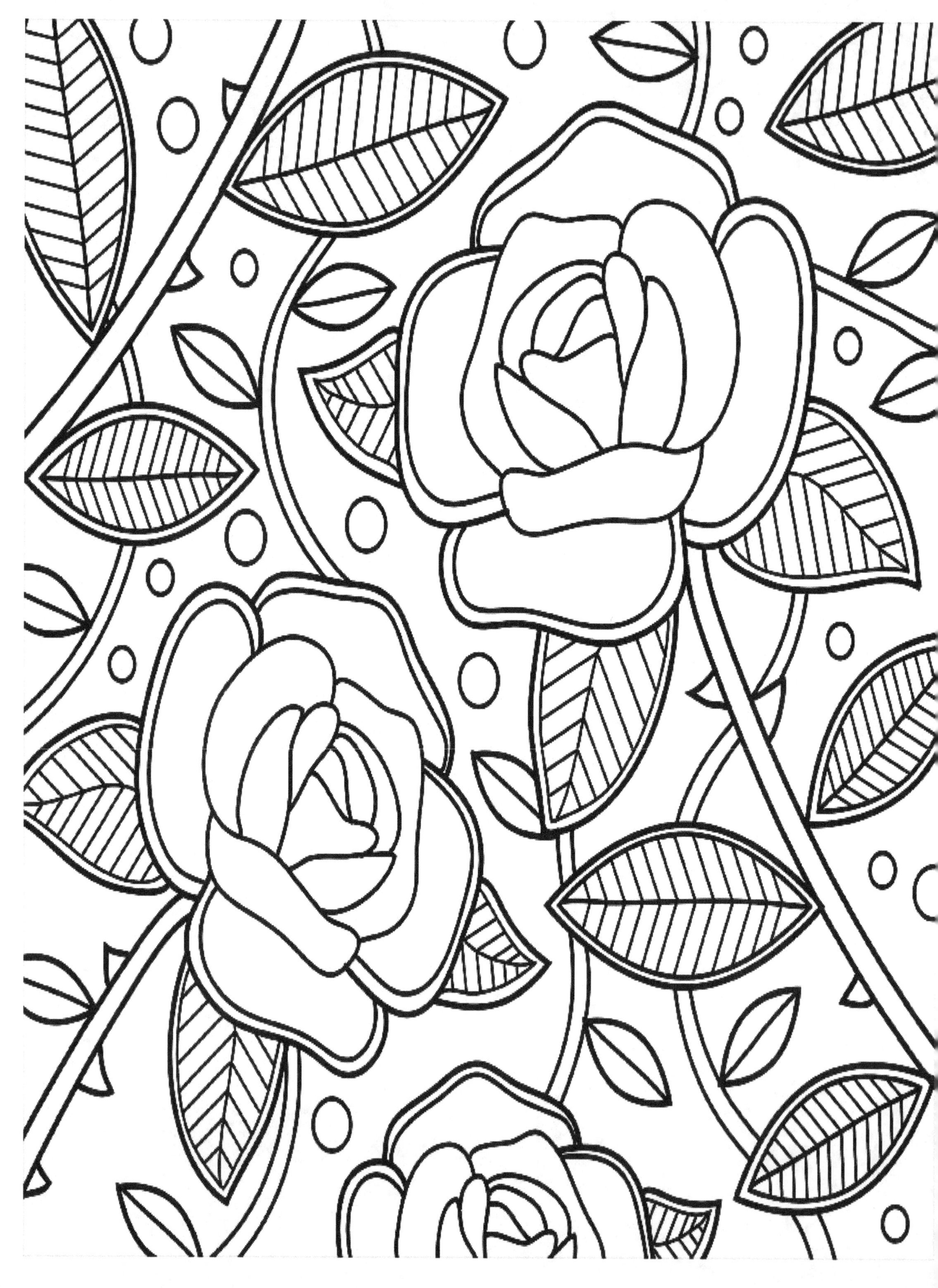

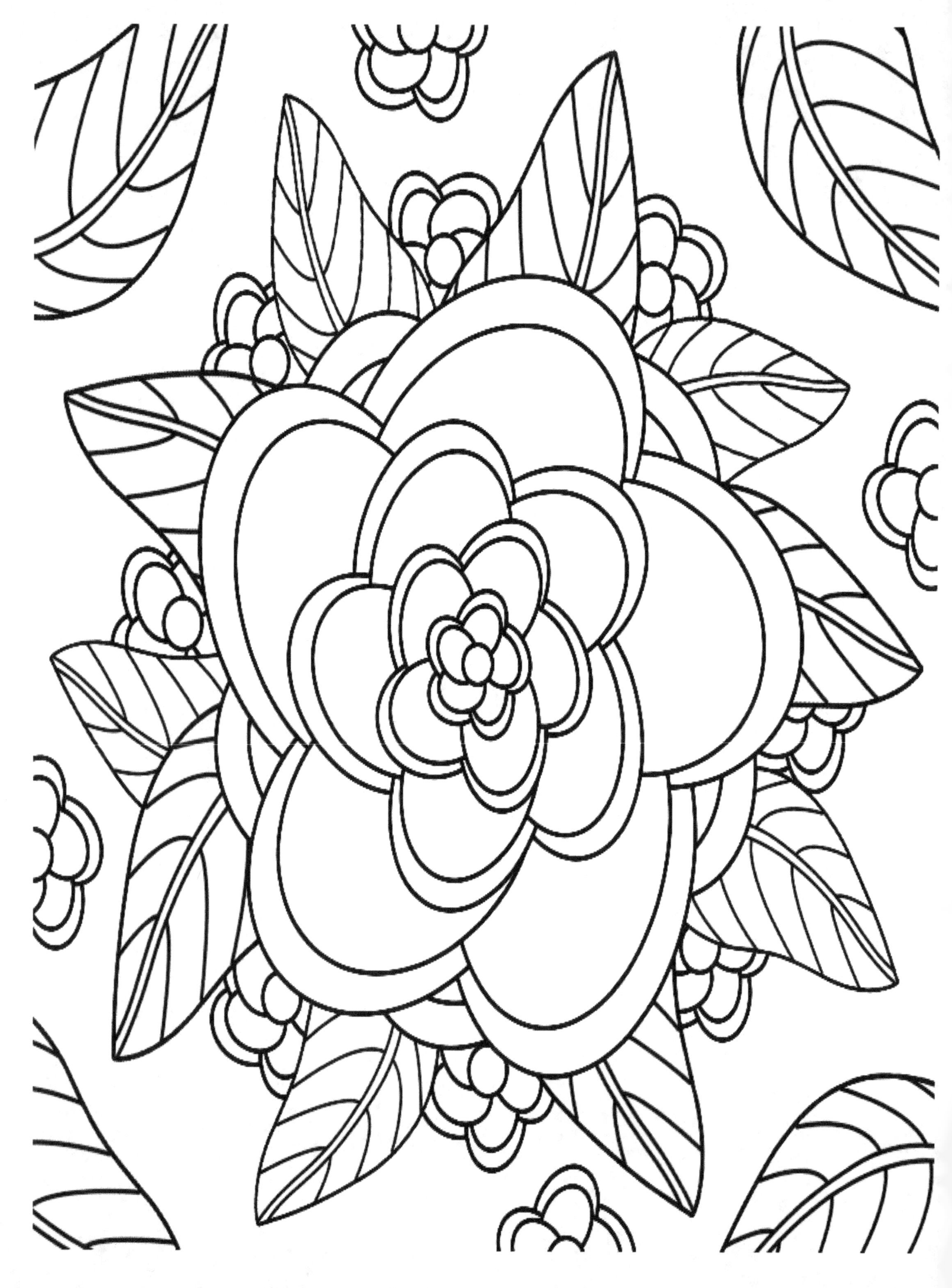

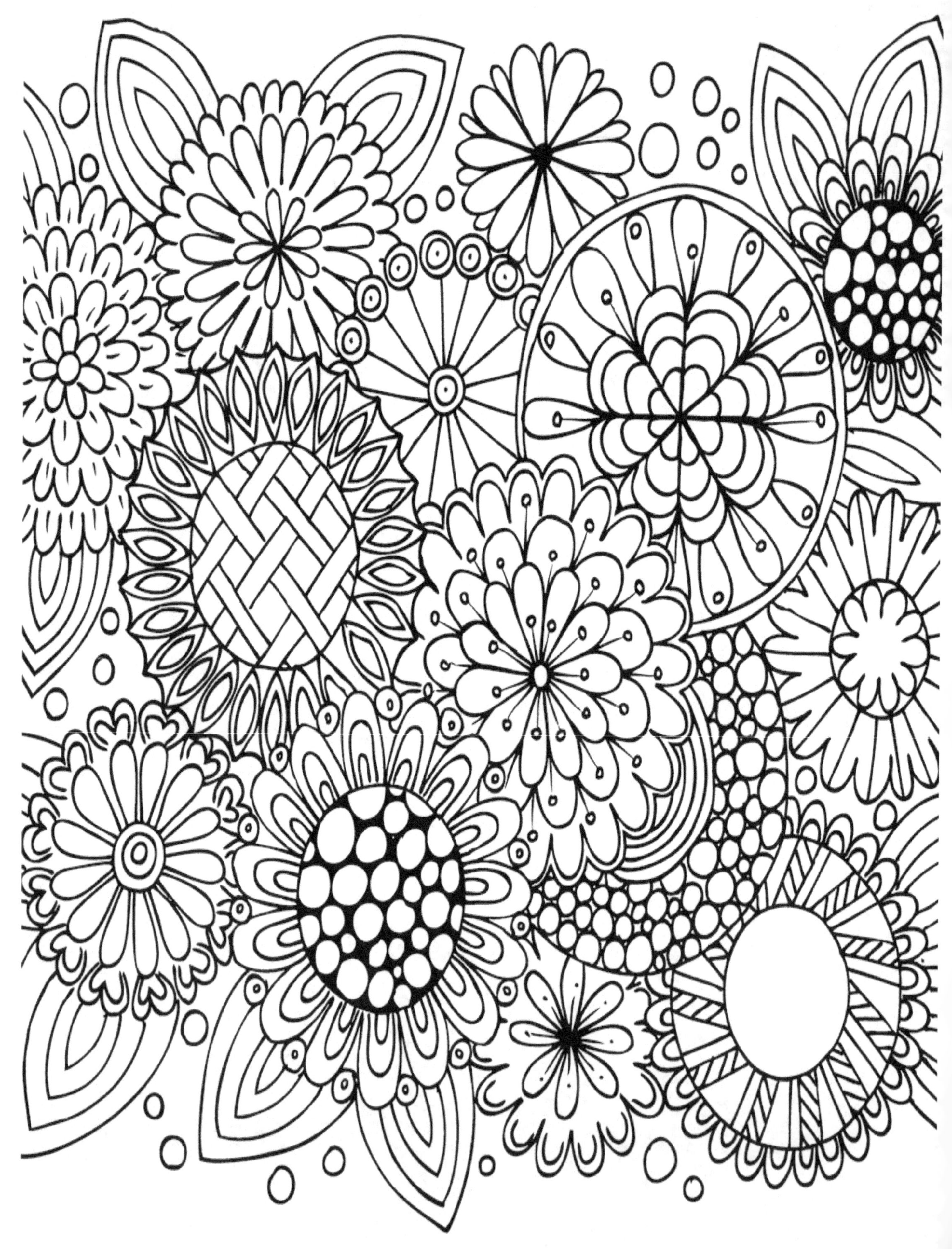

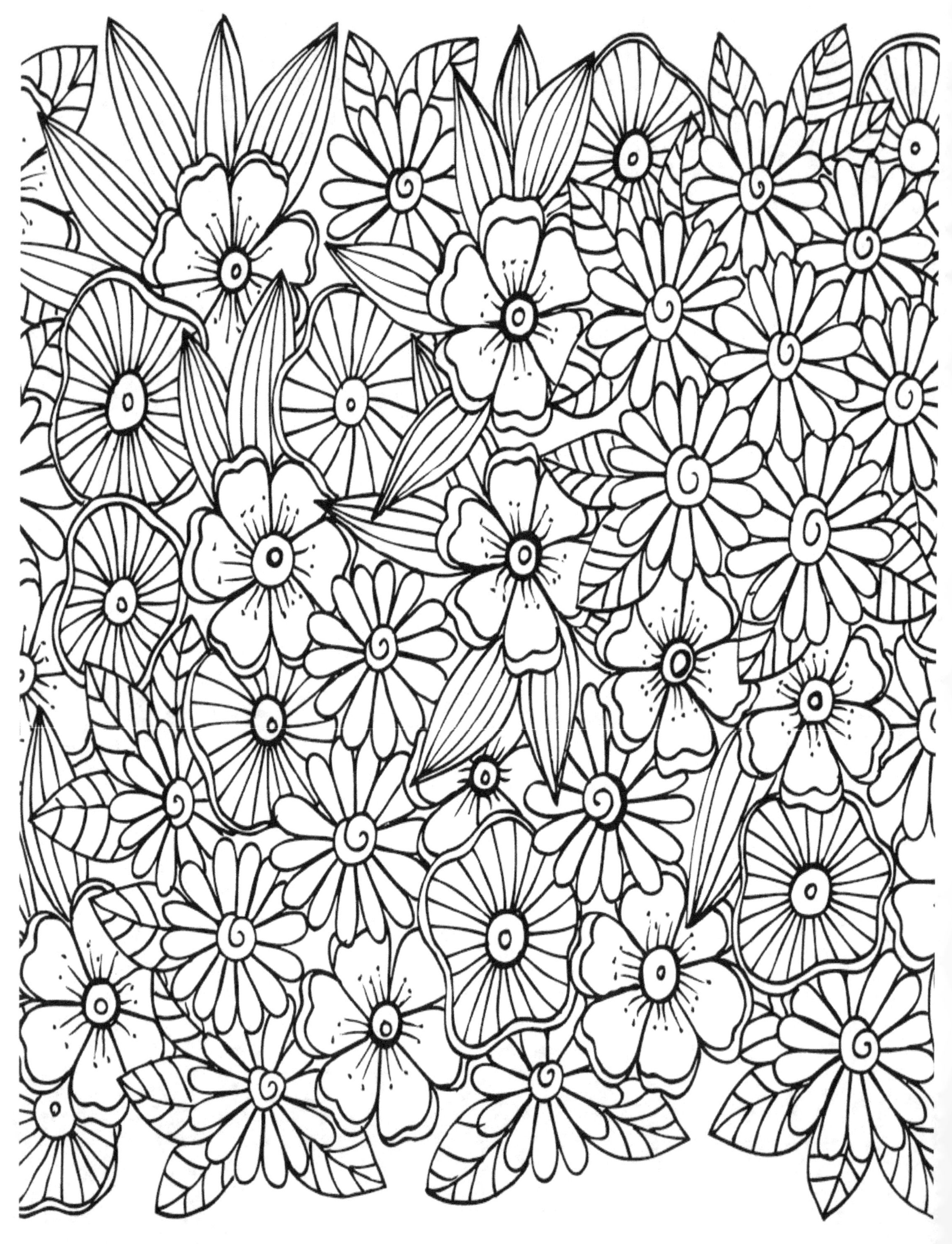

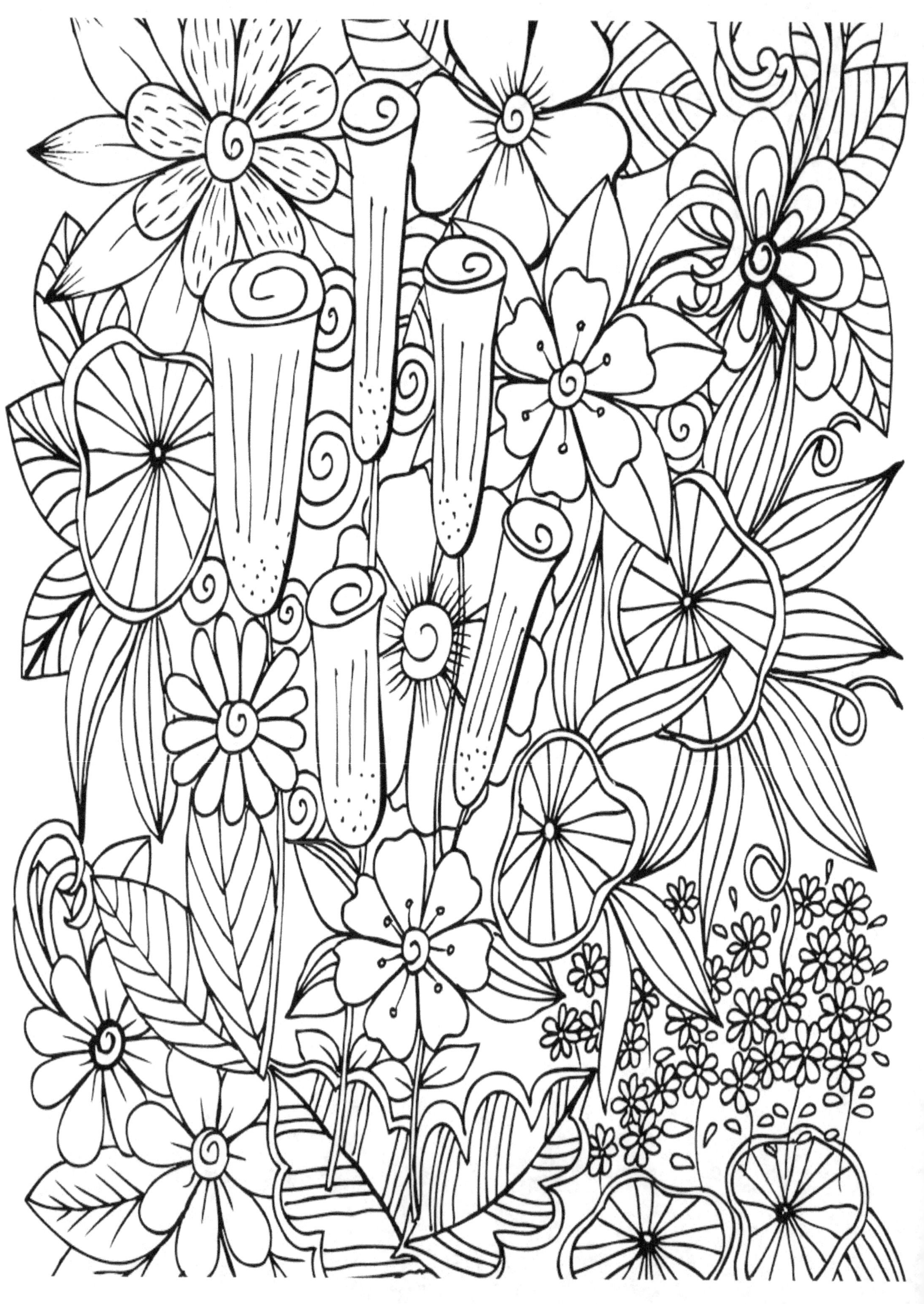

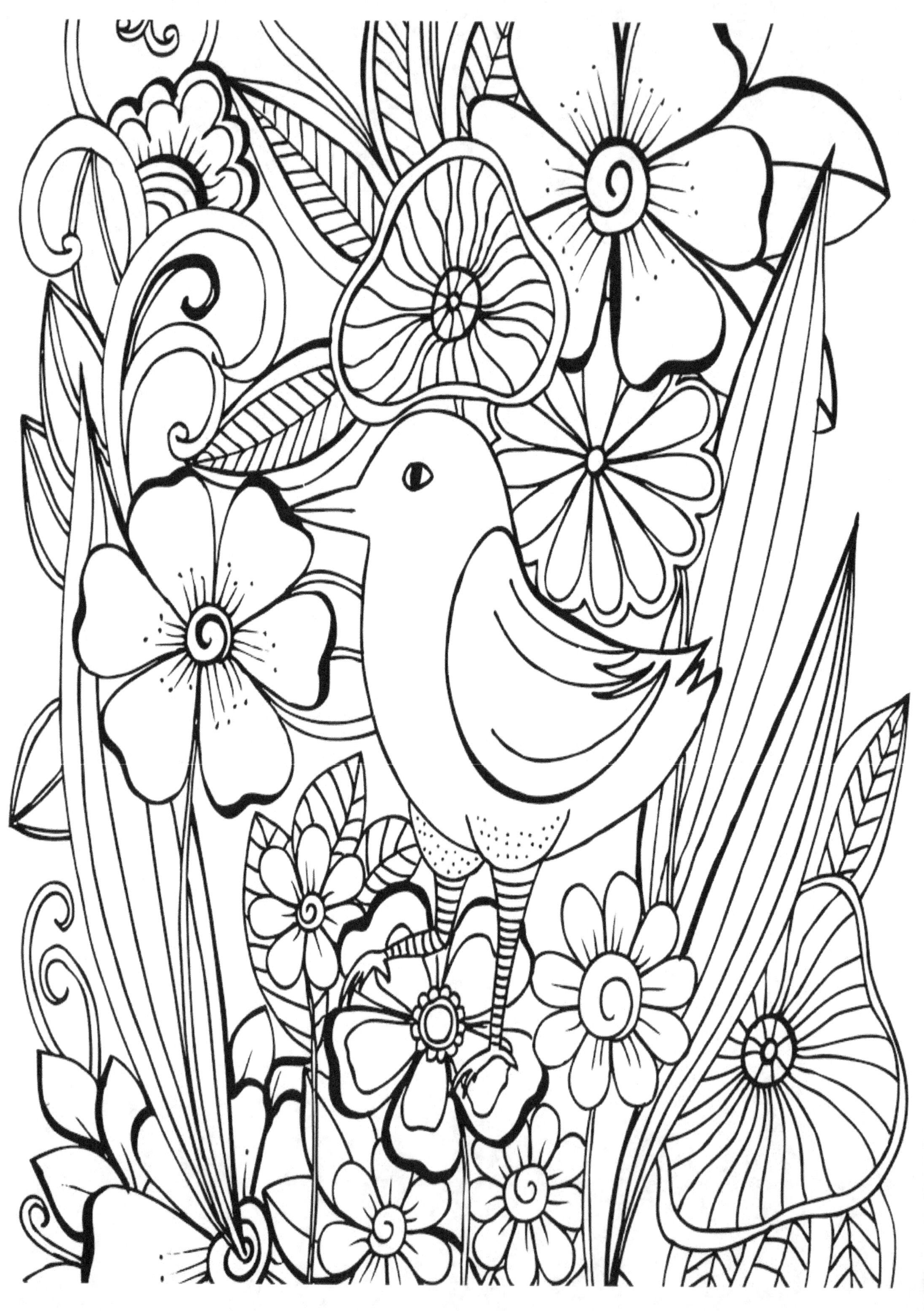

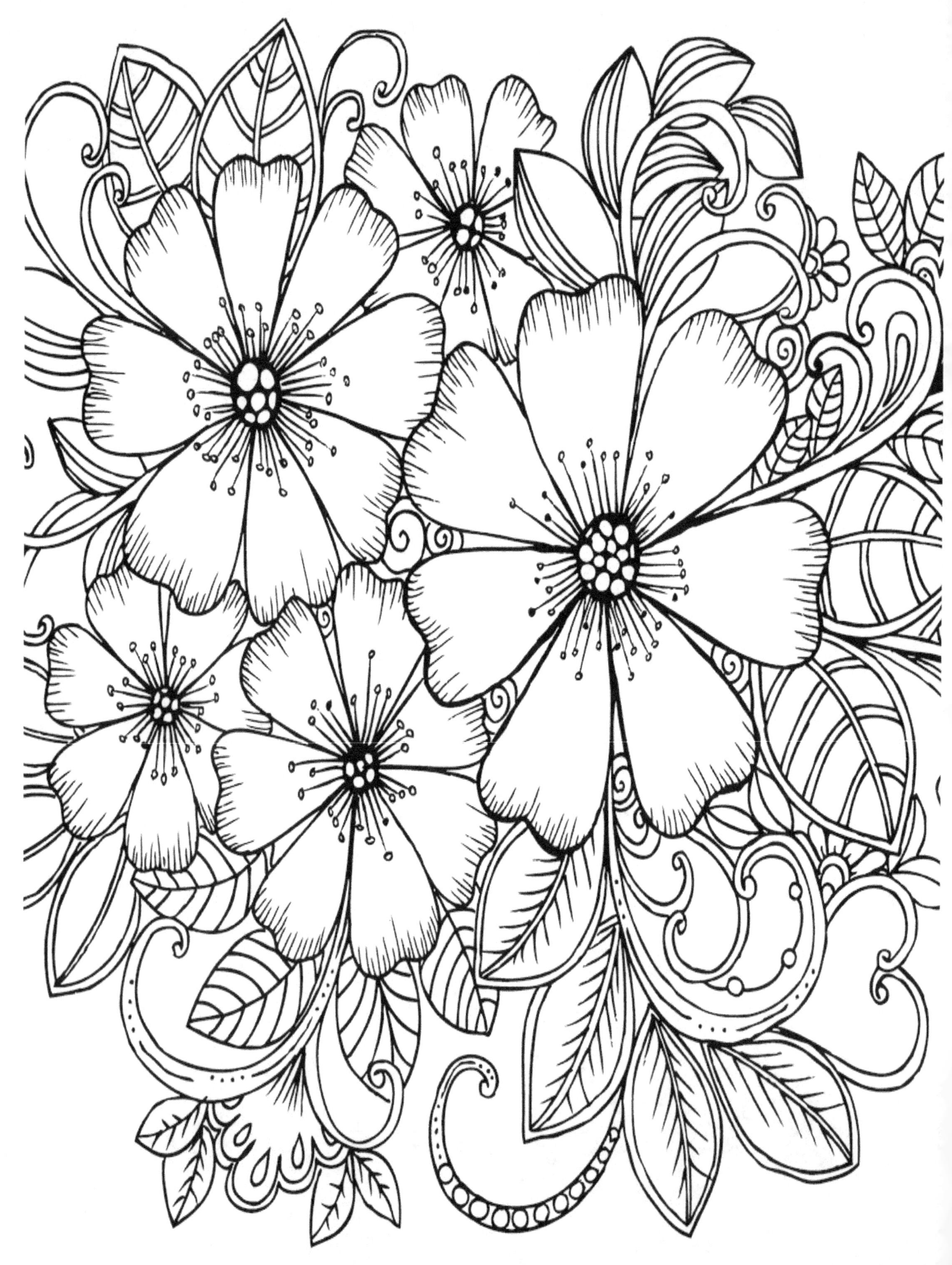

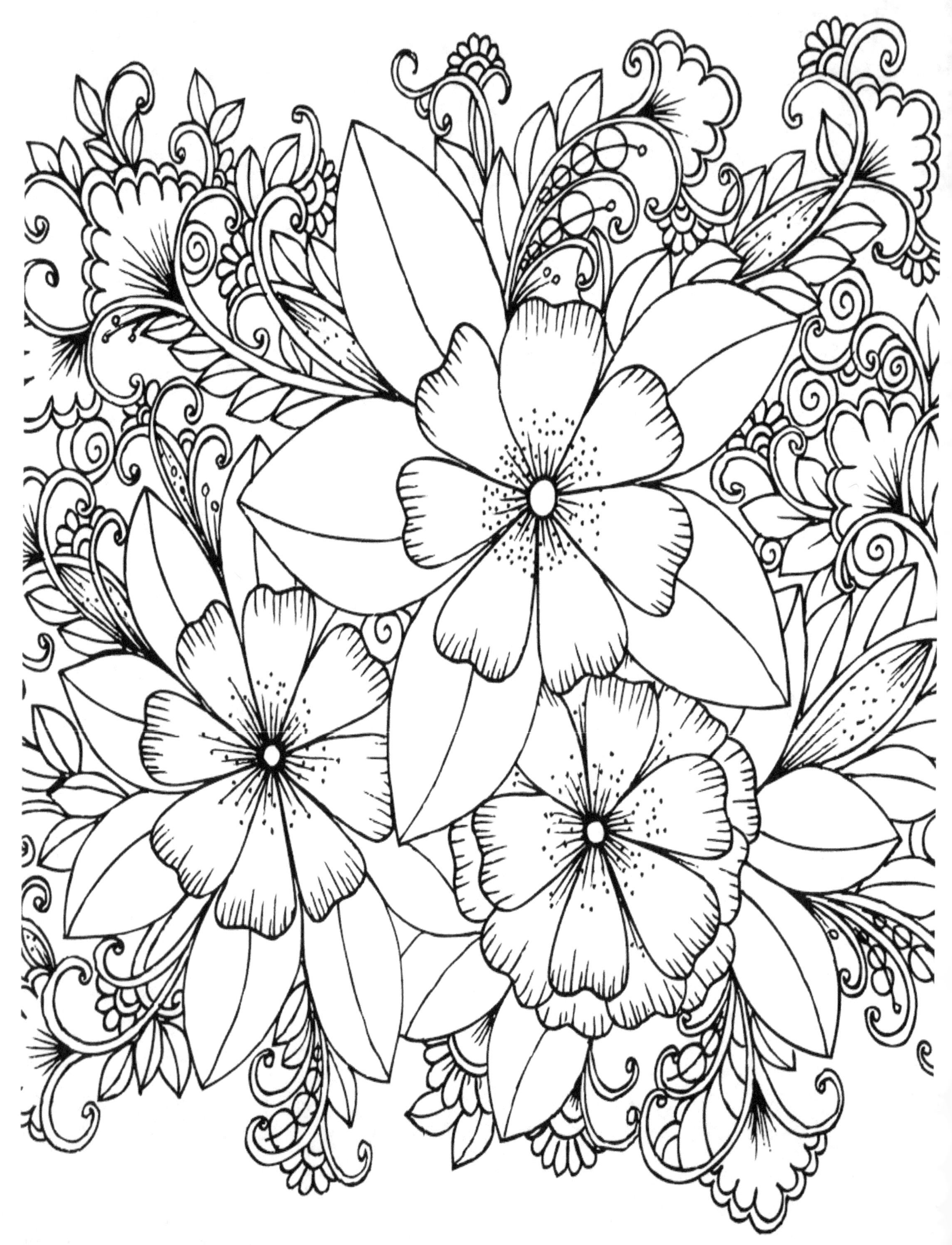

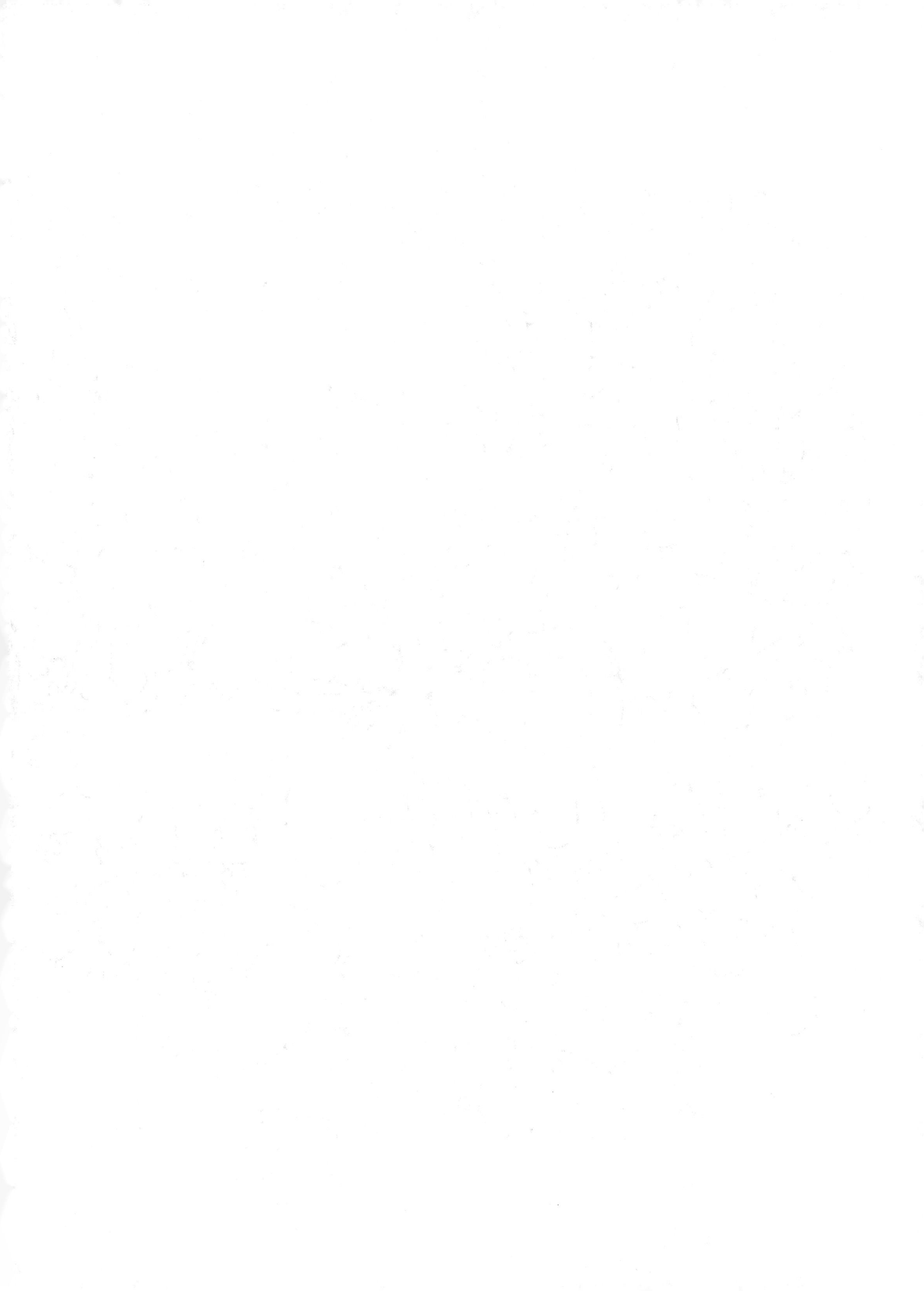

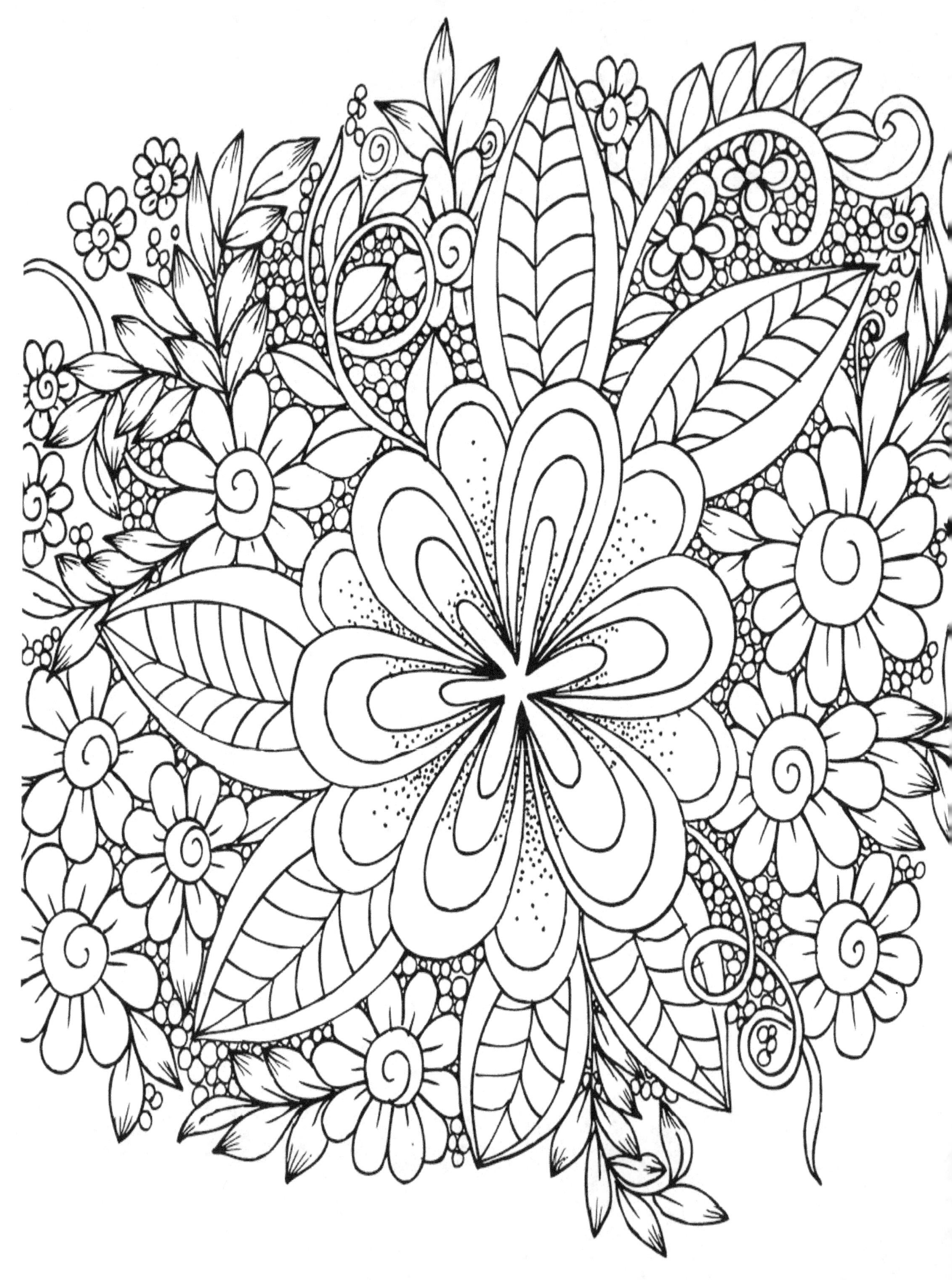

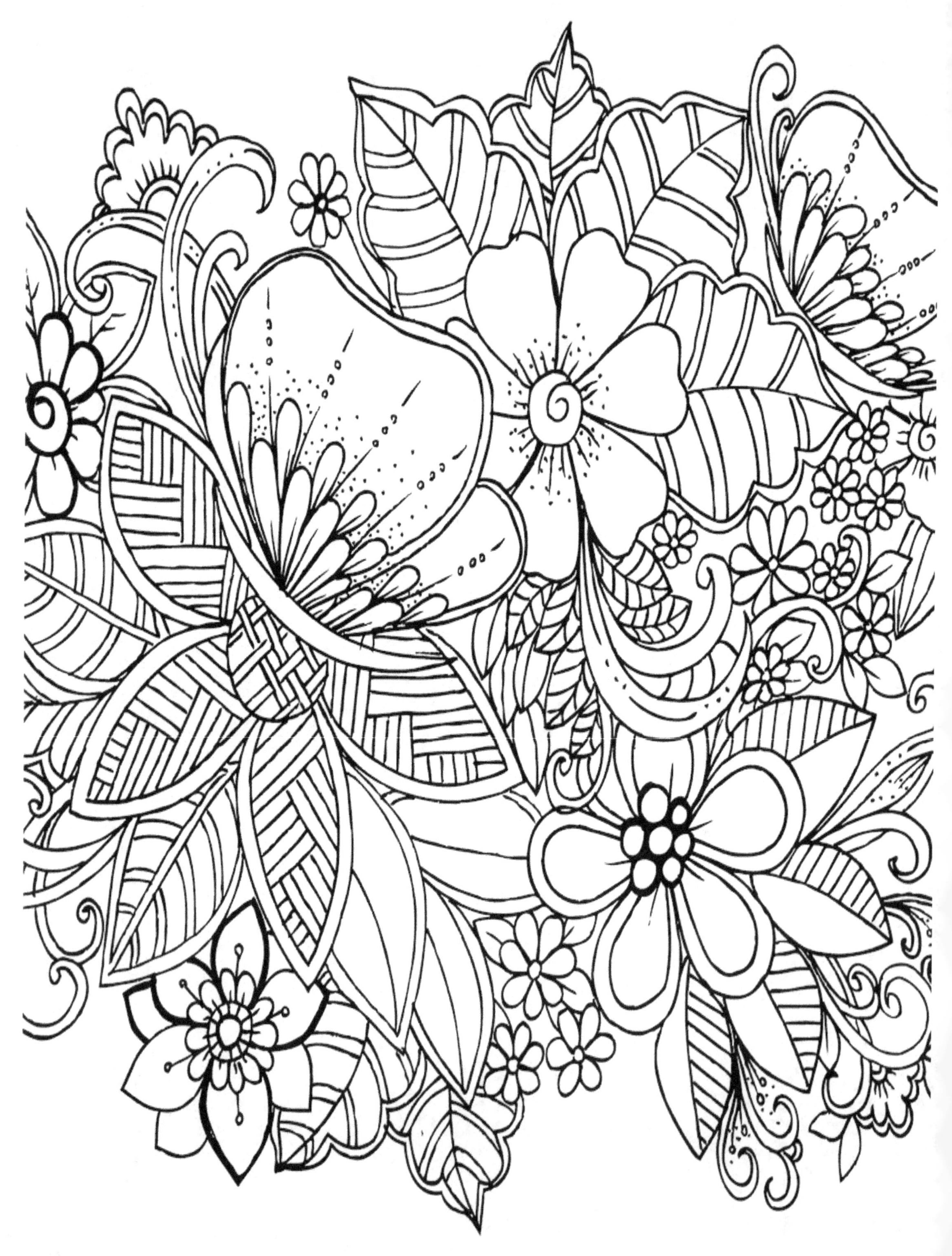

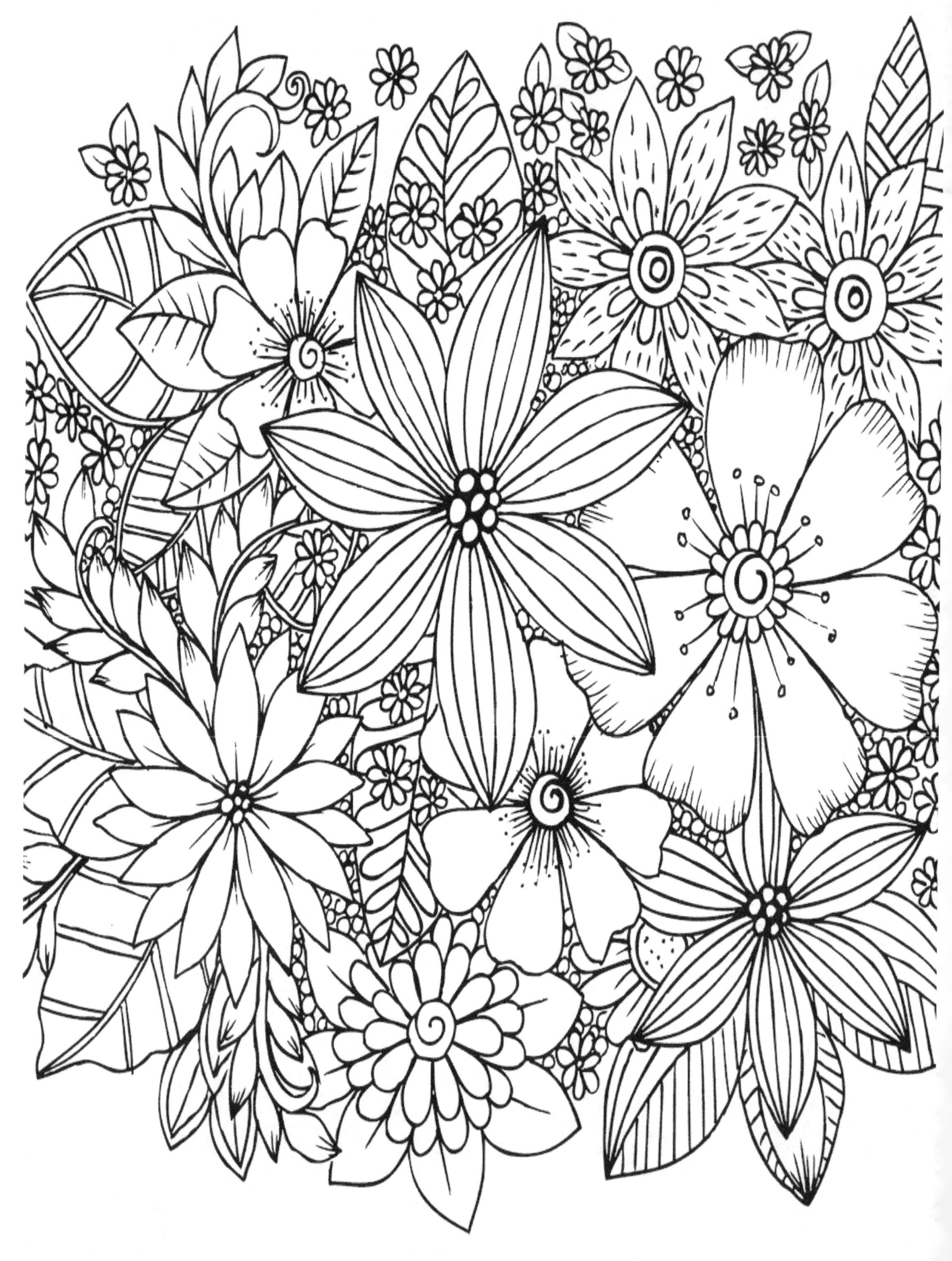

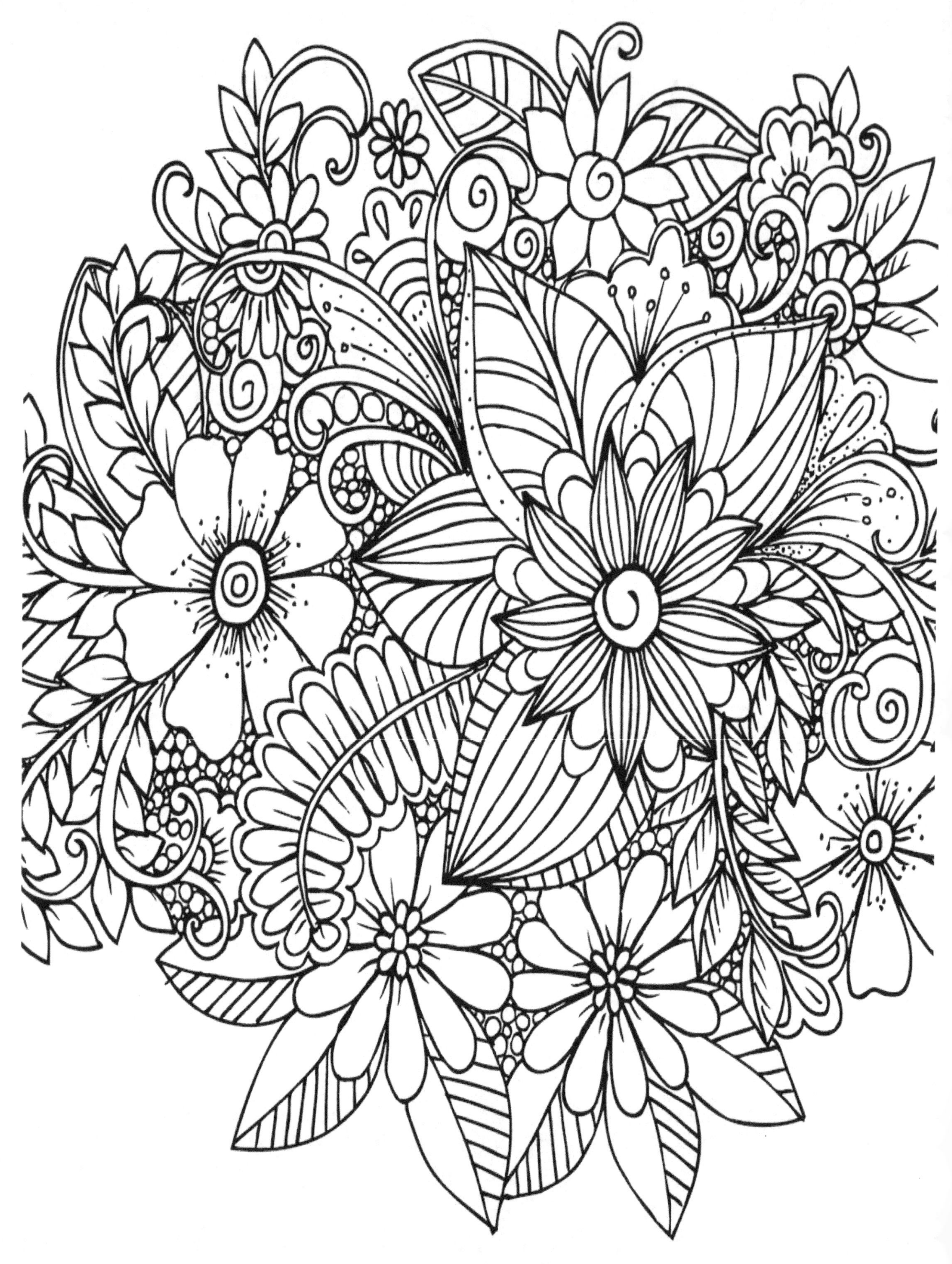

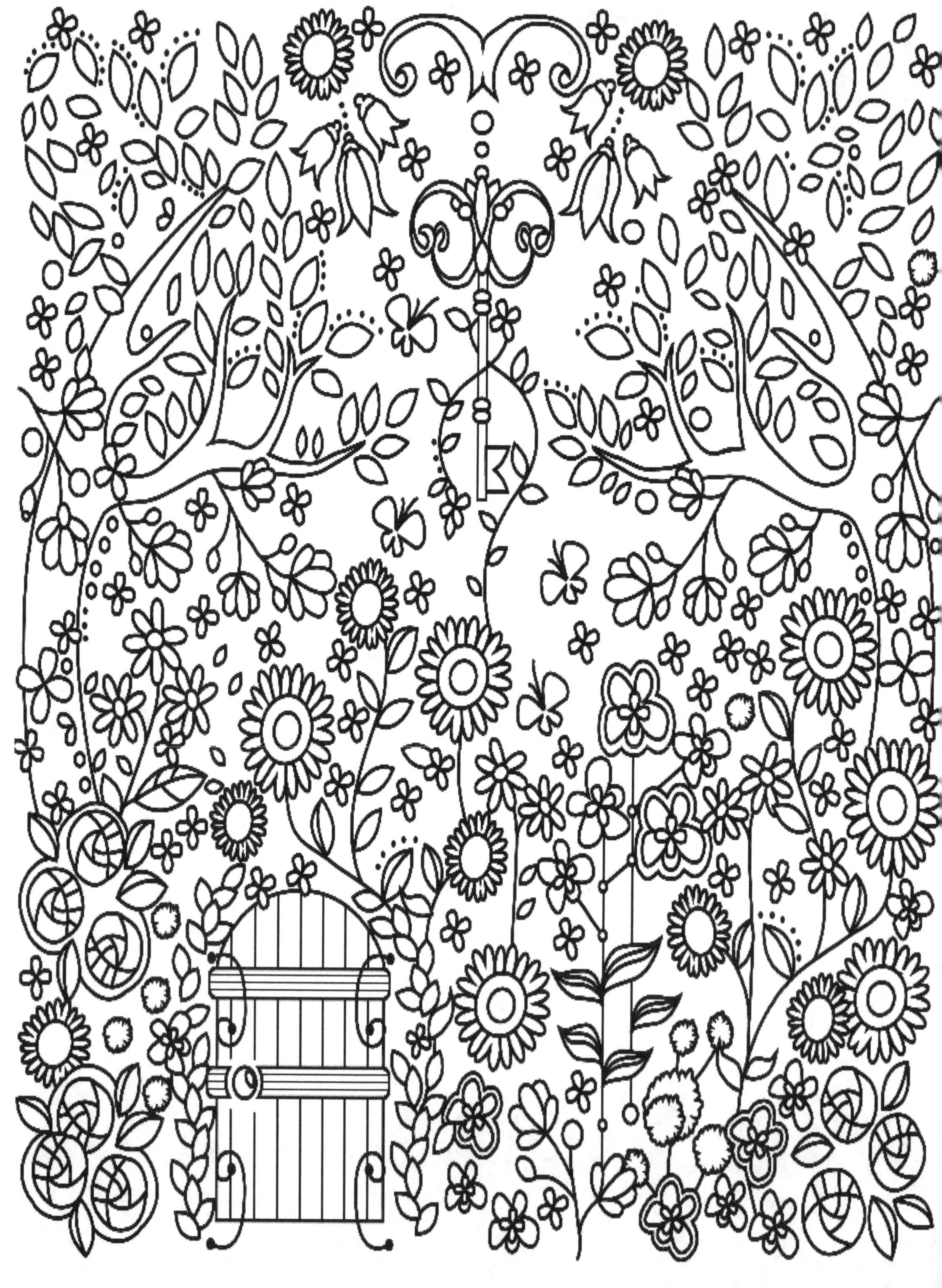

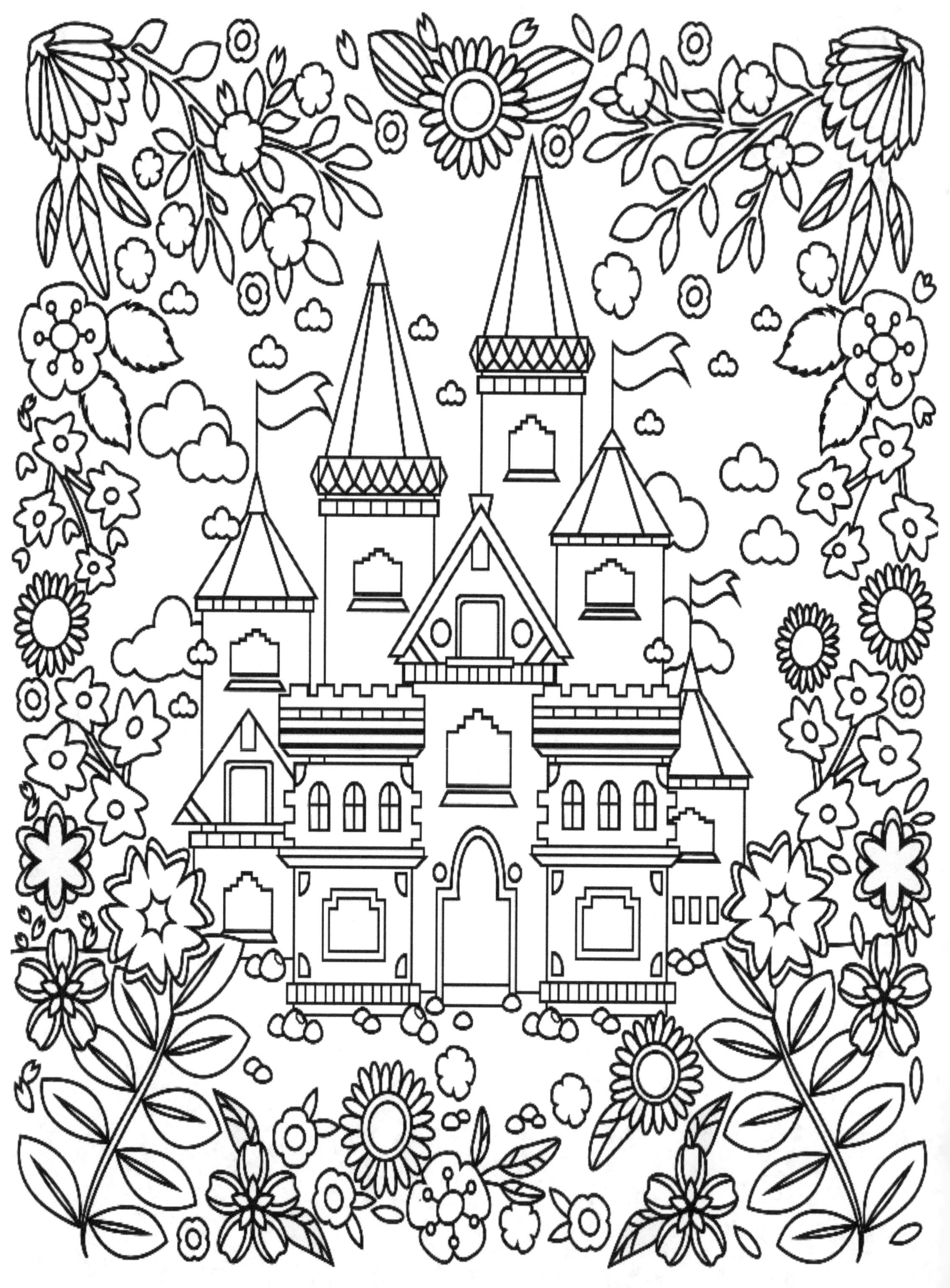

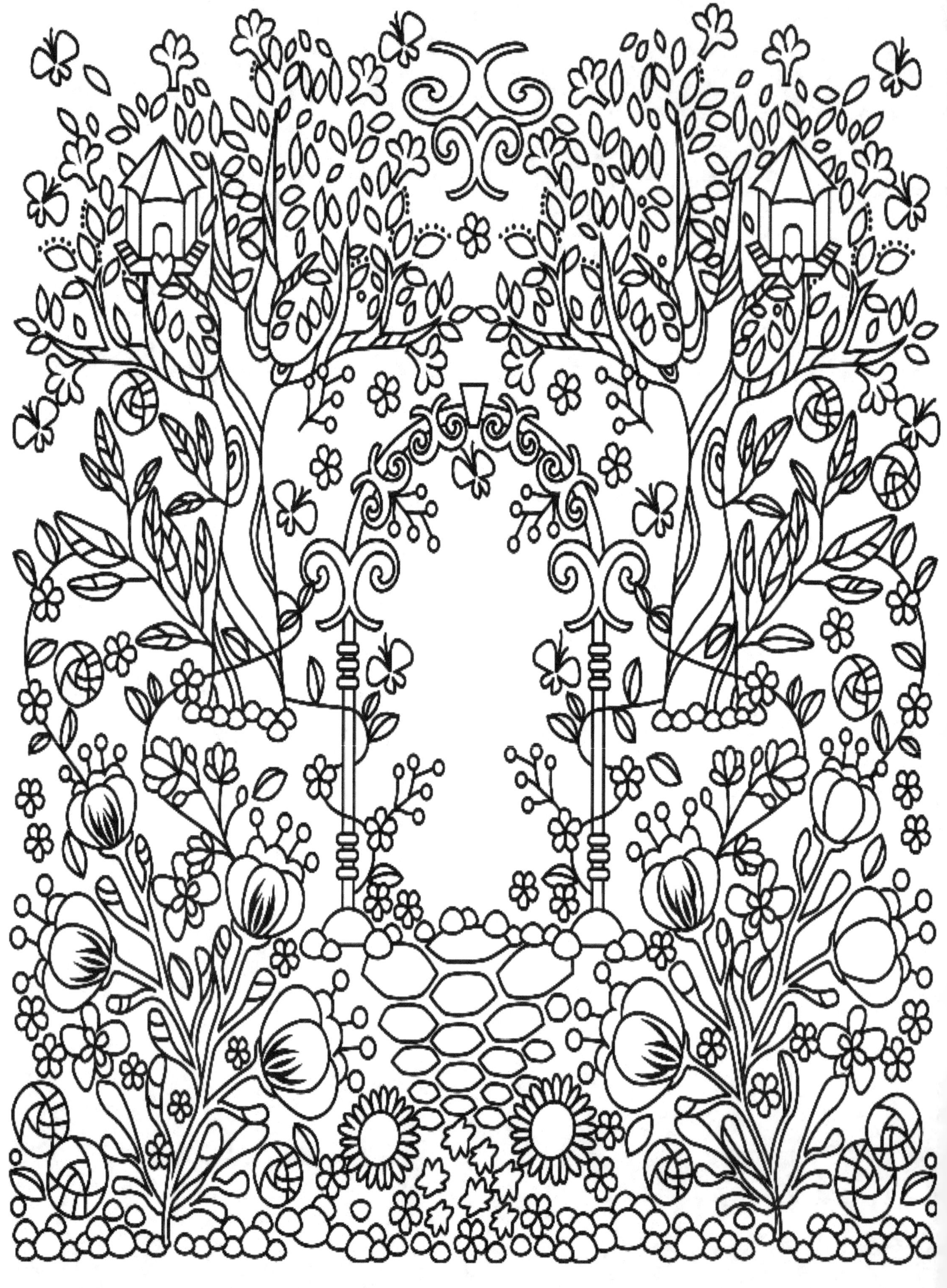

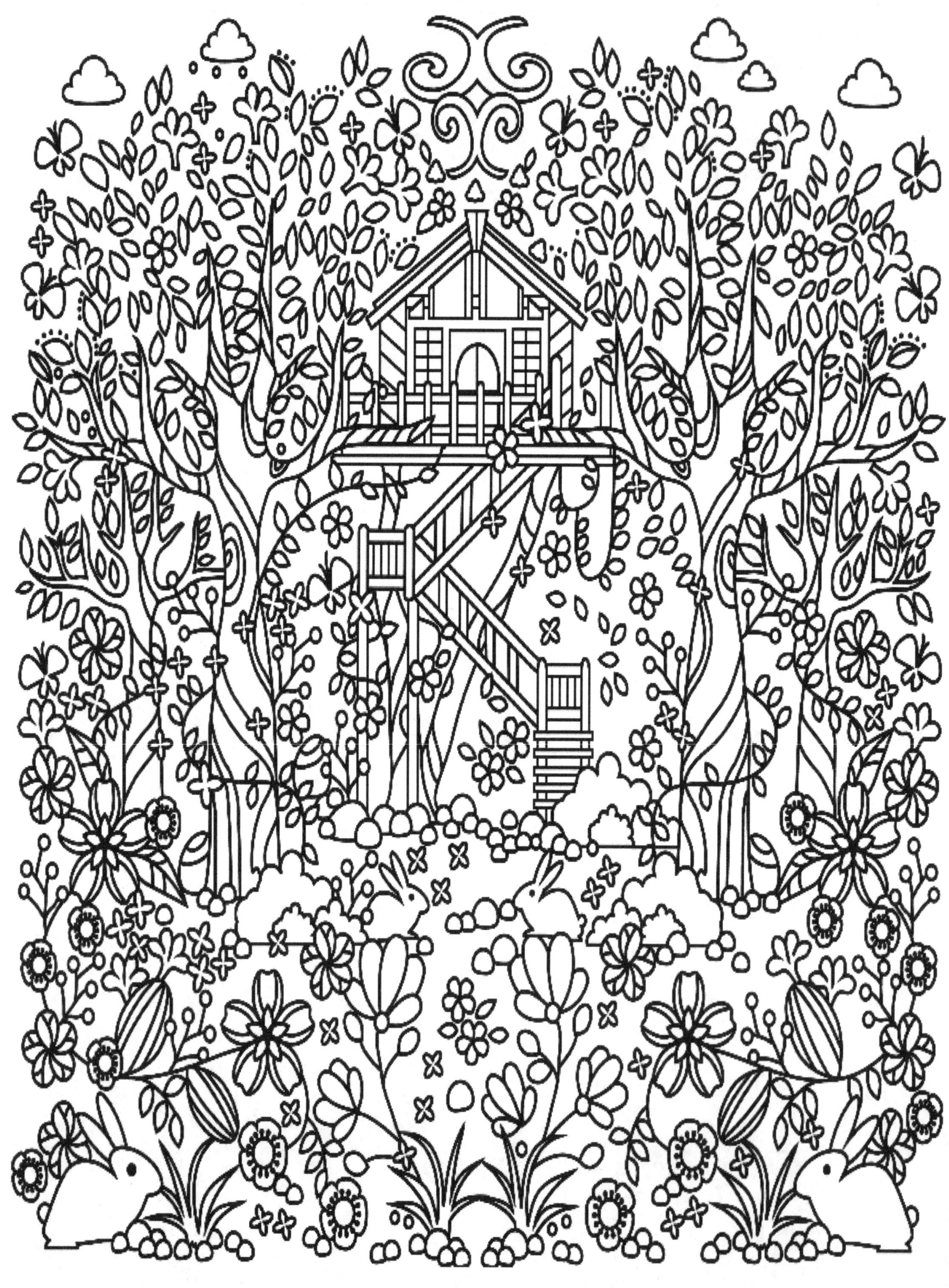

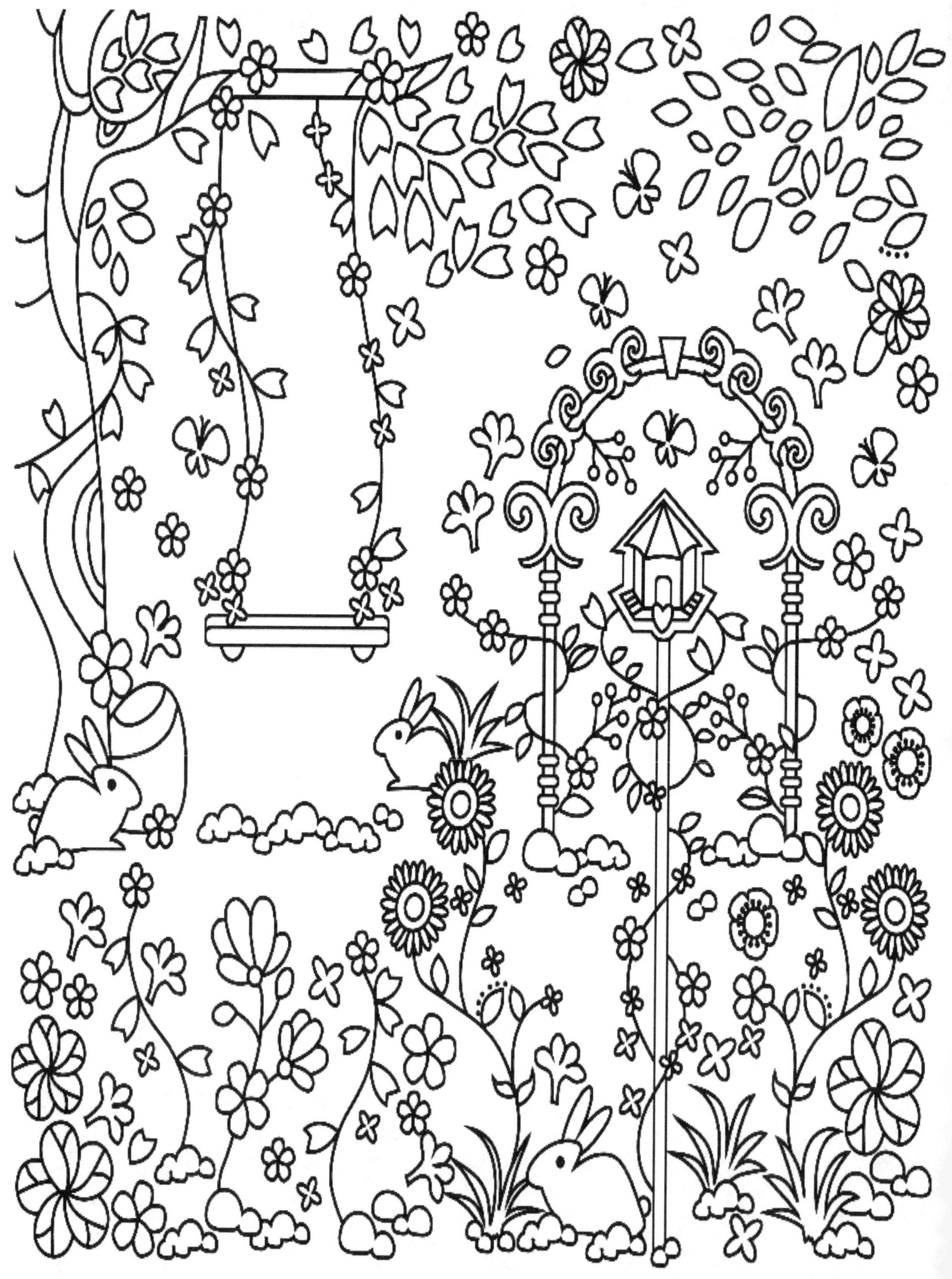

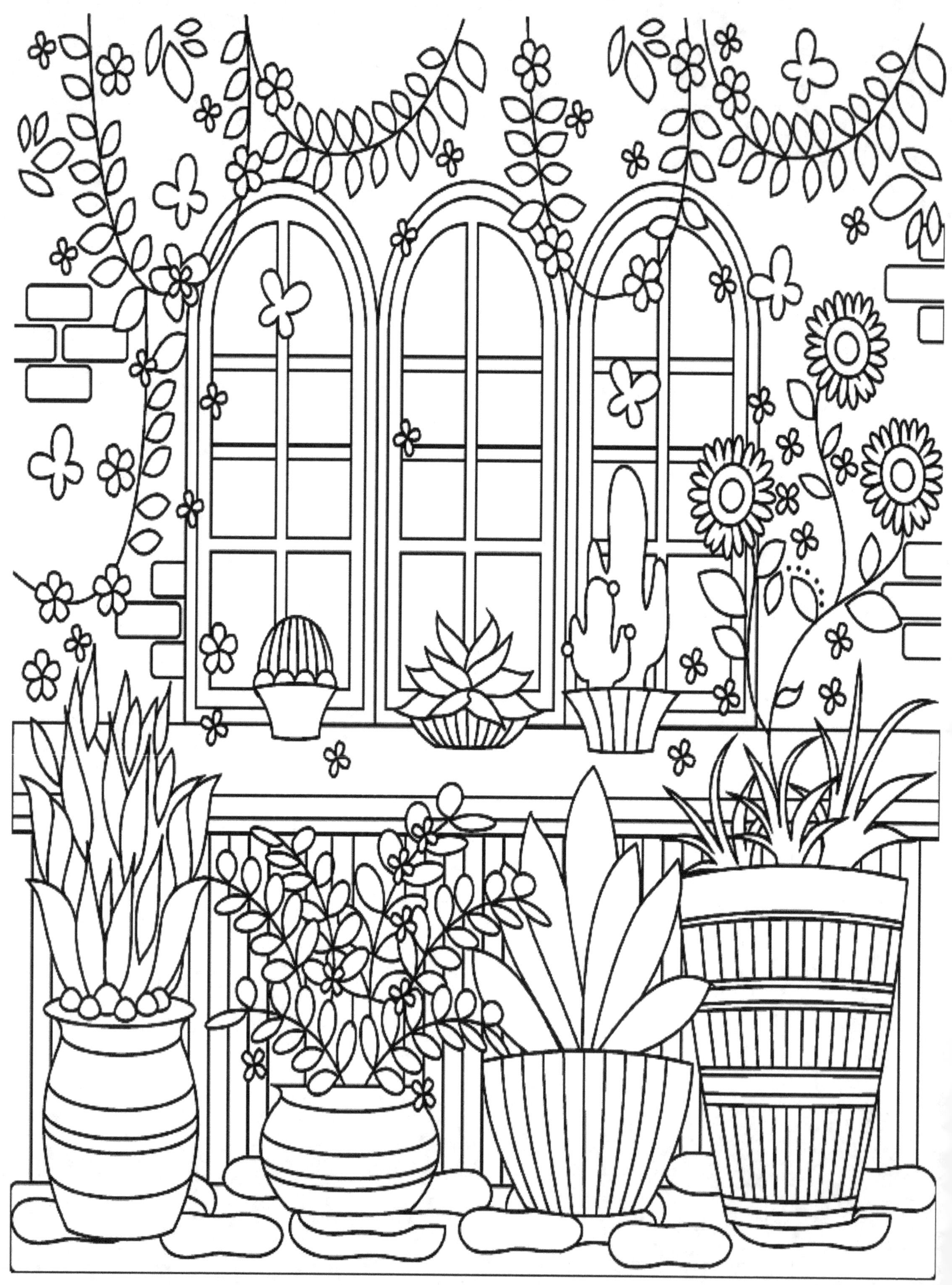